VICTORIAN AND EDWARDIAN
FIFE
FROM OLD PHOTOGRAPHS

VICTORIAN AND EDWARDIAN
FIFE
FROM OLD PHOTOGRAPHS

RAYMOND LAMONT-BROWN

AND

PETER ADAMSON

To David

Raymond Lamont-Brown

FOREWORD

BY

FRANK MUIR

THE RAMSAY HEAD PRESS EDINBURGH

Raymond Lamont-Brown dedicates this book to Gillian: and Peter Adamson to Iain, Gary and Hayley.

First published in 1980 by
The Ramsay Head Press
36 North Castle Street
Edinburgh EH2 3BN

ISBN 0 902859 69 2

Printed in Scotland by
Macdonald Printers (Edinburgh) Limited
Edgefield Road, Loanhead, Midlothian

Contents

ACKNOWLEDGEMENTS

The authors' grateful thanks are due to Ms Andrea Kerr, Curator of the Kirkcaldy Museum & Art Galleries, Mrs T. A. Jardine, of Cardy House, Lower Largo, Mr R. N. Smart, Keeper of Muniments, the University of St Andrews, and Mr Brown of Dunfermline Library, for assistance in tracking down some of the photographs in the collection—all of which are acknowledged individually as to source.

Particular thanks are due to Dr Frank Muir, former Rector of the University of St Andrews, for kindly writing the foreword to the book.

Photographic Sources

University of St Andrews: 2, 6, 7, 8, 9, 10, 11, 13, 16, 17, 19, 23, 24, 25, 31, 49, 51, 53, 74, 105, 106, 115, 121, 122, 142, 143, 144, 145.

Grafik Orzel Design Studio, "Lorimer Collection": Jurek Putter, St Andrews: 3.

Kirkcaldy Museum & Art Galleries: 5, 20, 27, 35, 36, 37, 38, 60, 61, 62, 67, 68, 69, 88, 90, 99, 100, 108, 110, 123, 124, 125, 128, 132, 136.

Mr G. Normand, Cupar: 56.

Mr J. Blythe, Freuchie: 14, 39, 42, 48, 65, 83, 126, 131, 137.

Mr A. H. Wilson, East Wemyss: 1, 30, 85, 87, 88, 95.

St Andrews Preservation Trust: 21, 22, 47, 50, 52, 57, 78, 86, 102, 103, 104, 127, 133.

Dunfermline Library: 34, 109, 111, 112, 113, 114, 118, 119.

Mr T. L. Rollo, Cupar: 12, 15, 77, 79, 82, 84, 107, 138.

Mr R. N. Smart, Strathkinness: 63, 120.

Mr J. Anderson, St Andrews: 117.

By Courtesy of the City of Dundee Museum and Art Galleries Department: 26, 33, 44, 46, 54, 55, 93, 94, 97.

Edinburgh City Libraries: 29.

Mrs T. A. Jardine: 28, 32, 40, 89, 140.

Cupar Library: 41, 91, 129.

Anstruther Fisheries Museum: 43, 45, 70, 71, 72, 75, 76, 96, 98.

Ceres Folk Museum: 58.

Mrs Mercer: 80.

Mrs A. Walters: 73.

Guardbridge Paper Mill: 64, 135.

FOREWORD

OF all the inventions of the last century which have impinged upon our private lives—and there have been a great many of them, e.g. bathrooms, bicycles, fish-knives, typewriters, cigarettes, etc.—perhaps none have impinged so deeply as have electrical gadgets and photography.

Once the nineteenth century inventors bent their minds to what to do with electricity they quickly had it jumping up and down and running along wires and leaping into the air without benefit of wires so giving us telephones, radio and television. All very useful and (occasionally) enjoyable but of no help at all to social historians. Speaking on the telephone became (occasionally) so easy and swift that nobody wrote letters to each other any more and so future ages will have no equivalent of the Paston Letters, or the correspondence of Mary Wortley Montagu or Dorothy Osborne or Horace Walpole to reveal to future historians how we today live and love and think, and what we endure and what we enjoy. Radio and television recordings might help a little but not, I fancy, much. The ironmongery of these gadgets is made obsolete so quickly by new technological developments that the tapes now in existence will not be playable on the machines of a few years hence. Officially important events will no doubt be transcribed on to the new forms of tape, or disc, or pill, but the officially trivial events and people—us and how we live—will be lost.

Photography, on the other hand, as this book ably demonstrates, stays put. A photograph, like a book, exists. All you need to read it is a hand to hold it and an eye to bring it into focus. What is more, within certain limits a photograph is truthful. Unlike a view or the depiction of an event drawn by an artist, a photograph has not gone through a process of being artistically or historically or politically edited in the artist's vision. If only the Tudors had invented photography I think that we would have a vastly different picture of how our ancestors went about their daily lives (my own mental image of previous centuries is based on the drawings of Rafael Sabatini).

Here, in this book, is a picture of how life was really lived in the Fife of Queen Victoria and King Edward. It is truth preserved by photography. Not the whole truth perhaps, because there is no such thing, but enough truth. These were the clothes that people wore. They lived in these houses.

The text by Raymond Lamont-Brown is an accurate and stimulating accompaniment to the splendid photographs of our beautiful, fertile, once so toil-worn Kingdom. But then the photographs were the responsibility of Peter Adamson who knows almost everything there is to know about the photography of old, interesting buildings (and ancient, crumbling Rectors).

FRANK MUIR

1. A tinker travels through East Wemyss in his distinctive "mobile shop"

INTRODUCTION

THE Victorian Age began at twelve minutes past two on the morning of June 20, 1837, on the death of His Majesty King William IV. In Scotland a transformation was to be wrought with the coming of his niece as the new monarch. This metamorphosis was to be readily felt in Fife at all levels of society.

The love affair which Queen Victoria was to have with things Scottish, did not embrace Fife. She was crowned at Westminster Abbey on June 28, 1838, aged twenty-one, and set foot in the ancient Kingdom of Fife at North Queensferry on Tuesday, September 6, 1842, during her first visit to Scotland. The Queen passed through Inverkeithing, the horses in her carriage were changed at Cowdenbeath, and she left the county soon after on her way to Kinross. That was the nearest that Fife was ever to get to a "royal visit." Thereafter she always sped through the county on her way to her beloved Balmoral.

From Dunfermline to St Andrews, the new Victorian architects quickly established their mark. Neo-classical houses and neo-Gothic churches began to jostle with the medieval and Hanoverian relics. Sound, functional, opulent Victorian dwellings were erected, which still stand as a memorial to the go-getting commercial prosperity of the period.

A stroll through the elegant squares and terraces, and past the white villas set amongst new planted trees bordering the parks in a Fife town in Victoria's day, would have shown true signs of increasing prosperity and expanding comfort. A turn down the unfashionable vennels and streets, abandoned by the owners of these new houses, showed a very different picture. The vennels of Fife were far more dirty, crowded and uncomfortable than they had been before the coming of Victoria. Alas no reflection of Victoria's "dear Paradise," as she called Scotland, was to be seen in Fife. The county had been caught in the vortex of the Industrial Revolution.

It was an age of flexibility, it was an era of social mobility. The advent of industry—from shipbuilding at Rosyth to papermaking at Guardbridge—had brought an influx of strangers looking for work; people who began to dilute the essential character of the Fifer. Accommodation became a problem; the old dwelling-houses from Tayport to Kirkcaldy were divided and sub-divided, so few Fife working men could boast more than two rooms for a prolific family. Dirt and overcrowding brought typhus and cholera in its wake. In 1848 plague struck St Andrews claiming 400 lives.

Because of the advances made in the west of Scotland in the cotton trade, the linen industry bacame concentrated almost entirely in Angus and Fife. Dunfermline remained a great linen centre, keeping its high reputation for damask, although the town's fabrics were greatly challenged by jute. By 1847 Kirkcaldy began to specialise in linoleum. Low wages and long hours were the rule in Victorian Fife. A linen worker was lucky to earn ten shillings a week, for a day which began at five thirty in the morning and ended at seven in the evening. The demand for juvenile labour was enormous; in 1865 only two-thirds of Fife's children were at school.

The swing from agriculture to industry continued steadily through the Victorian years in Fife. In 1801 thirty-one percent of the people were on the land; by 1901 it was four and a half

9

per cent. Fife agriculture, however, did not deteriorate in quality, though its economic fortunes fluctuated.

In the field of transport Fife was to have the glory of two "wonders." The great Tay bridge of 1878 was to end in disaster, as poignant photographs in this collection show; but the Forth Bridge was opened in 1890 as a great feat of engineering. More so, it gave Fife a key-link in the northward chain of transport.

From the early years of Victoria's reign a strange undercurrent ran through Scottish society. There was a broad and lively interest in things of the mind. This was to lead the country to be overschooled by the late 1850s, but the search for innovations and new slants on the arts was greatly encouraged. One art form above all others was to catch the imagination of the far-seeing Fifer—photography.

Fife's Role in the History of Photography

The County of Fife in general, and St Andrews in particular, was to witness the true birth of photography in Scotland. In this, the coming together of the talents of three men was to be important; those of W. Henry Fox Talbot, Sir David Brewster and Dr John Adamson.

William Henry Fox Talbot (1800-77), inventor, of Lacock Abbey, Wiltshire, had been educated at Harrow and Trinity College, Cambridge. He worked chiefly in mathematics and optics, and the chemical changes of colour; but, in 1840 he developed a new way to record likenesses—the calotype. From the Greek word for beauty, *kalos*, the calotype chemically developed images on paper, which had been sensitised with silver iodide and silver gallo-nitrate. The paper, exposed in a simple box camera for up to four minutes, "caught" the likeness. On removal of the paper from the camera it was developed as a negative by washing it again in silver gallo-nitrate. This negative was finally "fixed" with hyposulphate of soda (originally, a solution of bromide of potassium). For a lasting clarity the negative could then be treated with a coating of wax. Fox Talbot patented his calotype under the name of "talbotype" in 1841.

Fox Talbot was anxious that his invention should be popularised, for he wished for the recognition which had been accorded to the Frenchman Louis Jacques Mandé Daguerre (1789-1851), whose pictures on an iodised plate (daguerréotypes) had won him considerable fame. In order to advance his hold of the market, Fox Talbot approached Sir David Brewster to help find someone in Scotland to practise calotype commercially. Scotland, of course, was not hampered by the strict patent restrictions placed upon his inventions in England by Fox Talbot.

Sir David Brewster (1781-1868), Principal of the United College (1838-59), St Andrews, was an authority on the diffraction of light and had invented the kaleidoscope. A founder member of the British Institute for the Advancement of Science (1831), Sir David had followed Fox Talbot's experiments with great interest. A fascination which was shared by a colleague, Dr John Adamson. John Adamson (1809-70), who was to become Medical Officer of St Andrews in 1848, was a keen experimenter in photography, and produced the first calotype taken in Scotland. Following Fox Talbot's approach to Sir David Brewster, John Adamson's brother Robert (1821-48) gave up his engineering apprenticeship, ostensibly because of bad health, and began to learn the calotype process from his brother. So, sometime before the end of 1842 Robert Adamson had progressed enough to open the first calotype studio in Scotland at Rock House, Edinburgh. Incidentally the first commercial studio in Fife was probably the one set up in 1849 by Thomas Rodger in the vicinity of Pends Road, St Andrews.

Much admiring Robert Adamson's photographic skills, Sir David Brewster introduced him to the successful landscape painter David Octavius Hill (1802-70). This began the famous photographic partnership that, until Adamson's untimely death, was to produce some of the most beautiful, distinctive and characterful photographs in the history of photography. Their work won high acclaim and selections of their calotypes were exhibited at the Scottish Academy in 1844. Their collaboration was devised to bring out the best of the two men's talents: Hill chose the subjects and arranged poses, and Adamson handled the camera and developed the prints. Collections of their photographs sold right up to the 1880s when the snapshot began to become really popular. The collector's item, of course, is their volume entitled *One Hundred Calotype Sketches* (Edinburgh, 1848).

Hill and Adamson produced over two thousand calotypes, and firmly gave Fife the honour of being the place where the whole gamut of photography in Scotland was conceived.

The rise of the snapshot photograph

After the Frenchman Joseph Nicéphore Niepce (1765-1833) took what is generally accepted as the first photograph in 1826, coupled with the refinements of Daguerre, photography was very much restricted to the professional; or to the amateur who was prepared to devote much time and finance to develop the hobby. So between 1843 and 1878 there were few photographers in Fife outside academic dabblers. There were, of course, "itinerant photographers" who came to Fife, took rooms in a hotel and advertised in the local papers for custom. Usually this was a summer occupation. But the developing of photography in Scotland caught the imagination of many in the country, spurred on by such as David Octavius Hill.

Hill had become friendly with one Thomas Annan, a photographer and printer, whose family was to be much concerned with photography for decades. In 1883 the Annans brought the Klic process of photogravure to Scotland from Germany and rapidly exploited it. The Annans, like George Washington Wilson, court photographer to Queen Victoria from 1860, popularised the photographic view as house decoration. So few mantelpieces in Fife were not bedecked with a picture of the Queen and a pretty local view or two. Annan, and others, did appoint agents to practise in such Fife towns as Kirkcaldy, Dunfermline and Cupar.

John Thomson, the forerunner of the present-day photojournalists, James Clark Maxwell, the Scottish scientist who pioneered the colour theory, and John Kebble, the photographer who commissioned the world's largest lens in 1860, all contributed to the popularity of the photograph in Fife. But the cost and the difficult processes made it almost impossible for the man in the street to indulge in the hobby.

Then a London doctor, Richard Leach Maddox, proposed the system of the gelatine dry plate, and the commercial manufacture of photographic plates was made possible. By 1878 it was no longer necessary for the photographer to make his own materials. Thereafter new camera designs were promulgated until in 1888 George Eastman, of Rochester, New York, patented the first box form of camera. This transformed the practice of photography and thousands of ordinary people were able to develop the hobby and pastime. The "Brownie" camera of Eastman Kodak became very popular as did the folding camera. The camera shop as we know it today blossomed as a phonomenon after World War II. During the period of the scope of this book, camera equipment and processing was the area of the pharmacist.

Edward's Fife

The Edwardian Age began at six-thirty in the evening of January 22, 1901, when Queen Victoria died at Osborne House, Isle-of-Wight. The reign of the fat and fun-loving Edward VII was to be tinted with the sombre colours of his mother's reign; quite out of keeping with his character. While he was hailed as "Edward the Peacemaker," after his visit to Paris in 1903, his reign was a period of discontent and violence. Edwardian Fife reflected the bitter extremes of wealth and poverty, but witnessed the radical change and conservative reaction of social unrest.

By and large Scotland was still hostile to the name Edward, the race memory of the first Edward of England still being writ large. Yet, services were held in Fife churches when Edward developed perityphlytis, which caused his Coronation to be delayed. There were jubilations to mark the Coronation, but generally these were official junketings of school board and town council rather than a spontaneous outburst of enthusiasm by the people.

Throughout Edward's reign, Fife was staunchly Liberal, but the lifestyle of the representatives at Westminster was far removed from that of the people: a fact summed up in a remark made one morning by Augustine Birrell (MP for West Fife) while walking on the Raith Estate of Sir Ronald Munro-Ferguson, in company with Herbert Asquith (East Fife) and Richard Haldane. Birrell said: "What a grateful thought, there is not an acre in this vast and varied landscape which is not represented at Westminster by a London Barrister!"

The poor Fifer was much more introspective than his middle class contemporary. Family life still centred on the church, and social mores were ruled by a triptych of manipulators—the minister, the doctor and the schoolmaster. Faith was strong and radical. Asquith, the Yorkshire Liberal carpetbagger, recorded this of the Auchtermuchty electors as he went canvassing: "I can remember standing for more than an hour, after my first speech, while the old weavers in the audience put me mercilessly through every item of their Shorter Catechism of the Radical faith." Thoughts of higher things were an essential opiate to living.

Half the houses in Edwardian Fife had still one or two rooms with shared extra-mural sanitation. Most were dark, draughty, cramped, malodorous and vermin infested. A two-roomed house could cost as much as 3/6 per week, while a one-roomed cottage fetched 1/-; a high sum for an 18/- a week unskilled worker. Wages were by no means equitable for physical work done; a full-time maid-of-all work earned £30 per year, whereas a science master could command £140. But most people settled at the average 22/- a week fee of the farm worker.

The Edwardian period ended on May 6, 1910 when Edward VII died at a quarter to midnight at Buckingham Palace. By and large in that year the people of Fife were still earning less in real terms than they had in 1900. The ostentatious display of wealth and extravagance of Edward VII and his circle had left the lower classes resentful and dissatisfied; a feeling which was strong in Fife between worker and gentry. The year of the king's death introduced three years of civil strife in the United Kingdom of an unprecedented scale; strife which was felt at grassroots level in Fife.

A Fifer born in 1837 to die in 1910 would have seen many social changes. The spread of popular education, the enhanced mobility of new transport systems and the development of trade unionism, especially amongst the unskilled, made perhaps the most lasting effects. In Fife, too, were felt the movements which were gradually helping to forge Scotland into a single nation. The Liberal government's social and economic legislation gave Scotland a changing mood. Fifers felt themselves more Scottish after generations of considering themselves closer to the Anglo-Saxons of the south, than their Celtic compatriots above the Highland Line.

This book is aimed at being a distillation of Victorian and Edwardian social moods; it is a celebration too, of the part the county played in the history of British photography.

RAYMOND LAMONT-BROWN

CHAPTER ONE

PERSONALITIES AND CHARACTERS

PEOPLE'S characters change less than their outer surroundings. Yet in a world of two-dimensional people, we see today, in old photographs, what we would consider to be eccentricities of dress, little thinking of the singularity of action of the sitters, and why they became eccentric at all. In many ways the modern welfare state—heralded on January 1, 1909 with the introduction of the Old Age Pension of 5 shillings (25 pence) a week for all over seventy years of age—has stifled eccentricity. Again such august bodies as the Royal Commission on the Poor Law and the Relief of Distress, and subsequent legislation, has swept away the dirt, squalor and ill-health that bred bizarre and abnormal behaviour. The horrors of poverty of Victorian and Edwardian Fife—hunger, disease, overcrowding and insanitary environments being only a social crust—bludgeoned the weak and helpless into an erratic crankiness difficult to understand today.

Once Fife streets teemed with curious folk, many doing jobs that are with us no more, like lamplighting and knife grinding. The itinerant workers and street characters rubbed shoulders with those of different eccentricity: the pursuers of middle class social pretensions and the upper working class obsession with "Sunday best outfits." The rich and aristocratic were less interesting in their eccentricity; their social position gave them a kind of community licence to oddness that was an accepted norm anyway.

Such as "Caum" Eppy (plate 10), as pictured in the wonderful Lawrence Swan Thomson Collection of the University of St Andrews, was typical of the street character of the day. When she walked, the upper part of her body was bent parallel to the ground. Eppy always carried a key, which she averred was the "Key to Hell." Famous for her pawky wit, Eppy received her nickname from the slate pencil (caum) used to whiten a hearth or a doorstep.

Because of the university at St Andrews, many a famous character was drawn to Fife, exhibiting eccentricity of genius. Yet the beauties of the county were a further attraction, particularly to those of literary bent. R. L. Stevenson spent some time (1868) at Cunzie House, Crail Road, Anstruther. In his "Random Memories" from *Across the Plains* (1892) he says "he lodged with Bailie Brown in a room filled with dry rose-leaves." In the evenings he wrote "Voces Fidelium," dramatic verse dialogues inspired by Fife's ambience. To Kirkcaldy Thomas Carlyle came—he lived in Kirk Wynd, off the High Street, and taught at the Burgh School (1817) for £80 per year—and formed a firm attachment to the county.

A great friend of Carlyle's was the individualistic Balie Patrick Don Swan (1808-89). A flax-spinner, Swan bought St Brycedale House in 1850 and was Provost of Kirkcaldy at different times over a span of thirty years service (see plate 20).

2. Dr John Adamson

3. Thomas Rodger

4. Principal Sir David Brewster, KH

5. Operators with early stereoscopic camera

6. "Draughts," 1861. John Brown with his two sons, John and Thomas.
A classic early composition.

7. The Playfairs, representative of the early posed studio style calotype

8. Early Victorian "Conversation Piece," near St Andrews Cathedral

9. Water Landscape Study, 1862. Ivy Bridge, Leslie Den, Markinch

10. Caum Eppy, 1860, by Thomas Rodger

11. Mrs Murry of Crail, in her 101st year, 1859-60

12. Sunday promenaders, St Andrews, 1890. Note the wheeled bathing machines on the West Sands.

13. Jamie Spence and Bos'on Tamson, prominent stone masons in St Andrews, 1860

14, 15. Contrasts in costume. Compare the working class costume of the Falkland worthies with that of the fine ladies of Cupar, below, 1900.

16. The characterful Professor Day, who held the Chair of Medicine at St Andrews, 1849, by Thomas Rodger

17. Itinerant Tyrolese street players, well known in Fife in the 1880s

18. An early attempt at cartooning, using a lampoon on the characters in the annual
Kate Kennedy procession at St Andrews

19. "Equal before God." St Andrews middle class churchgoers of mid-Victorian years.

20. Thomas Carlyle on the steps of St Brycedale's, Kirkcaldy. On the extreme left is John Carlyle (TC's brother); next to TC is Mary Aitken Carlyle (TC's niece), and Provost Swan. By then Swan was rich and famous, but in 1817 he was a pupil of Carlyle's in Kirkcaldy Burgh School.

21. "The Daftie" William Trail, 1865.
He was a newsvendor in St Andrews

22. "The Pilot," Walter Fenton, who lost his leg
at the Battle of Trafalgar, 1805

23. Two well known Cupar characters—"The linties" (lamplighters)

24. "A bit crack." A celebrated character study of the two St Andrews worthies, McKibben & Gairdner, and the latter's daughter.

CHAPTER TWO

PLACES

AS would be expected, photographs of Fife from around 1840 to 1910 are not numerous. Those which have survived are frequently found to be in a poor state of preservation. Alas the bonfires lit by next-of-kin "clearing up" the property of deceased relatives have robbed us of much of our local photographic heritage.

Our immediate reactions to old photographs are probably threefold. There is initial pleasure in a rather superior assessment of "how quaint" our ancestors were. Yet there are feelings too of horror at the economic depravity of the social content of some pictures, and how hostile the faces of the underprivileged seem with the passing of several decades. Then, there is the alarm to be felt at how the artefacts of whole generations have been swept away in the pursuit of "progress."

What exactly do old photographs tell us beyond the obvious? If one recognises the commercial round of portrait views for what they are, those deliberately posed plates show us exactly what they purport. They display people in their surroundings in the best way possible of illustrating life as it was. It was a world in which man was at the helm of creations. Yet the contrasts between city and country illustrate some of the main social problems of the Victorian and Edwardian ages. Herein can readily be seen the "two nations" of the country as defined by Conservative Prime Minister Benjamin Disraeli (1804-81) in his political novel *Tancred* (1847).

The photographs show the great contrast and variety in Fife and those chosen here are of exceptional interest. Victorian roads seem perpetually coated with mud, dirt and horse manure: it would undoubtedly have been a noisy world too, with hobnails on paving and the rattle of steel-rimmed wheels. After 1900 or so wood blocking for roads was begun and the introduction of tarmac improved the surfaces.

Sometimes in the old photographs it is difficult to hit on a date. Often clothes help in dating, sometimes buildings, but in pictures of towns and villages in Fife there is often little change in surroundings from Victorian to Edwardian days. Nor did country folk follow fashion. Clothes that looked as if they might belong to the 1870s were still being worn in some places up to the 1920s.

Particularly, Victorian photographs emphasise a number of facets: there is a prevalence of children; the clothes of the poor look uncomfortably thick and were undoubtedly infrequently cleaned. All in all there is an impression of an industrious, hard-working people, dressed overwhelmingly in shabby solemnity.

Victorians are shown to take life seriously even in the most beautiful of surroundings. There is scarcely a smile to be seen on any face, each is disciplined to the conventions of the period. Most are so unrelaxed that the expressionless faces give no clues to thought and feelings. As the reign of the fun-loving Edward VII developed smiles came to the posed photograph; only to be swept away again at the coming of World War I.

25. Cantilever Railway Bridge over the Forth during construction 1882-90, looking towards Fife shore. The bridge is 8291ft long with two main spans of 1710ft each.

26.   Street at Markinch, 1897. Note the unmade road surface and the open drains.

27.
Portion of Rosyth
Village. Early
pre-fabricated
dwellings.

28. Fisherfolk in festive mood at Lower Largo, birthplace of Alexander Selkirk (1676-1721), original of Daniel Defoe's *Robinson Crusoe*. The photograph was taken in 1885, when Selkirk's statue was unveiled. The quotation in the picture is taken from a traditional rhyme.

Traditional Largo Rhyme:
O weel may the boatie row, and better may she speed;
And weel may the boatie row, that wins the bairns bread.
The boatie rows, the boatie rows, the boatie rows indeed.
And happy be the lot of a', that wish the boatie speed.
I cuist my line in Largo Bay, and fishes I caught nine,
There's three to boil and three to fry, and three to bait the line.
The boatie rows, the boatie rows, the boatie rows indeed.
And happy be the lot of a', that wish the boatie speed.

29. Inverkeithing Tollbooth Cross, 1856, by Thomas Keith.

30. Very early photograph, c. 1840s, of East Wemyss by Thomas Keith

31. Largo harbour and viaduct from Drummochy, from a calotype by Thomas Rodger.
    The first trains ran here in 1856.

32. Lower Largo Beach, c. 1900

33. Culross town house and square, c. 1890

34. Dunfermline's cobbled High
    Street, looking towards the
    Townhouse, 1880

35. Dysart Town Hall. The stone over the arched doorway is dated 1576; a stone on the staircase is dated 1617. Photographed before the police buildings were added in 1920s.

36. Kirk Wynd, Kirkcaldy, with Upper Hendry Hall and the Old Kirk

37. Roadworkers in a busy Kirkcaldy street, c. 1890

38. Old Salt Pans, 1900. Premises of Thomas Reilley, Salt Manufacturer.

39.
Roof Trees of William Smith's house
in High Street, Falkland, 1903. The
unusual architectural trees were
removed to the palace.

40.
"Auld Robin Gray's" cottage, near Kilconquhar. Gray was a herd at Balcarres. He was immortalised in the ballad "Auld Robin Gray" by Lady Anne Lindsay (1750-1825), daughter of General James Lindsay of Balcarres.

41. East High Street, Elie, 1904

42. Cross Wynd, Falkland, looking towards the Parish Church and Bruce Fountain. A fine nineteenth century "atmospheric" conversation piece.

43. West High Street, Elie, 1884. Note the variety of wheeled transport.

44. Crail Harbour, May 12, 1894

45.
Cellardyke, 1910.
Most folk cleaned the
paving outside their houses.

46. Ceres Church, April 28, 1896. This had been built on the site of the
13th century church in 1806.

47. Fisherboys across the burn from the 13th century church of St Monance.

48. Strathmiglo, Townhouse & Steeple.
    Near the home of Eppie Ramsay.

49. The remains of Blackfriars Chapel, and Madras College, 1865. The Dominican monastery was founded here by Bishop William Wishart (1272-79).

50. Back of the Royal George, St Andrews harbour

51. The entrance gateway to the cathedral precinct, called the Pends; it dates from the 14th century.

52. North street looking west, and old Fisher Houses

53.   The West Port, St Andrews, re-built 1589

54. The church of St Athernase, Leuchars.
Built by the crusading di Quincys, the church was dedicated in 1244.

55. Parasolled ladies pose in tippet and bombasine at Newport School, 1886

56. Mercat Cross, Cupar, 1903. The lamps were melted down in World War II.

CHAPTER THREE

OCCUPATIONS

EARLY photographs of people enacting daily occupations in Fife are rather rare. Two reasons for this present themselves. First, an exposure time of several minutes was needed and the working man had little time to spare to wait around. Again, before the invention of the dry plate, to take a camera out into the fields and byways was a cumbersome operation, involving the haulage of a considerable weight of equipment.

Some delightful pictures do exist like Plate 79 showing Mary Rollo of Cupar making butter and the Kirkcaldy boys making shoes (plate 67). A very interesting picture is Plate 81, which shows Thomas Berwick. He was photographed in September 1893 in the Botanic Gardens of St Andrews University; the site of the original garden was where the Bute Medical building is today. Berwick assisted J. H. Wilson, Lecturer in Botany 1888-90 (and his successor Professor R. A. Robinson, 1890-1935), to lay out the garden in 1889. The garden was opened to the public in 1890.

Because of the importance of the fishing trade in Fife in Victoria's day there are many photographs of fishermen and the redoubtable fisher-lassies recruited by the fish curers. The work was seasonal (January-March/Summer/October-December) and payment was in gold sovereigns. Many of the fisher-lasses worked eighteen hours a day (Sunday was an official rest day), were mostly itinerants and lived in the cheap boarding-houses of the East Neuk. An important repository of relics of fisher folk in the East Neuk is the Anstruther Fisheries Museum.

Victorian Fife still presented a wide range of different trades from chimney sweeping to shipbuilding, and from basket making to cobbling; even by 1910 the old crafts of carpentry, stonemasonry and iron working were still flourishing. The colliers, tramps and gipsies of the photographs underline the great poverty of late Victorian Fife. Pedlars too were once common, catering mostly for the children of the workingclass.

Population has accurately reflected the changes in occupations, particularly the depression in agriculture. By the turn of the century more women were to be seen working in the fields, and the Fife factories depended upon cheap female labour. The Liberal Prime Minister Herbert H. Asquith was to feel the brunt of these women's tongues when he was first adopted candidate for the East Fife constituency in 1886; a facet that was to dog his political life as the suffragettes later made him a prime target.

These old photographs reflect some interesting trade changes. The pace of life was very much slower and the pursuit of material wealth was substantially less than it is today. Each shop had its staff of delivery boys and many establishments kept open until about eight in the evening. Definite changes too were seen in shop fronts. In Victorian times the modest bow-windowed shopfronts were swept away to make way for vast expanses of plate glass. In towns there was a return to the medieval trader idea of having a goods overspill outside shop doors.

57. The postie arrives, St Monance, c. 1898

58.   The family village grocer. Ceres, c. 1905

59. Carpentry lesson aboard the *HMS Mars* while moored in the Tay

60. George Barn, saddlemaker, Kirkcaldy, 1903. The site of his shop
    is the present-day Littlewoods.

61. "Puzzle Wullie"—a pedlar selling home-made toys and puzzles. Kirkcaldy, c. 1908.

62.
Caledonian Linen Mills,
Kirkcaldy, 1900.
Packing and
Despatching Department.

63. Counting and packing paper, Guardbridge Papermill

64.
Guardbridge paper
workers and their
foreman. Few working
men went bareheaded
in this era.

65. Woman spinning, Falkland, c. 1889. Hand-loom weaving and spinning was still a cottage
industry in such places as Auchtermuchty and Falkland up to the 1890s. A great deal
of linen yarn was brought to these landward towns from Kirkcaldy port.

66. The last town crier of Crail.

67. Kirkcaldy boys making shoes, c. 1860. A working week of 90 hours was not unknown.

68. Victoria Battery, 1898, Kirkcaldy. Guncrew of the 1st Fife VA.

69. Salvation Army Band, Kirkcaldy, 1900

70. Mrs Tarvit, expert fish cleaner, St Monance, 1910.
Note the bandaged fingers, protection against the sharp gutting knives.

71. Staff of the Cross Keys Hotel, St Andrews, c. 1900

72. Fisherfolk in North Street dwellings, St Andrews, 1890s

73.
Fisherwoman, with
herring basket,
nurses child.
East Wemyss, 1910.

74.
"When the boat comes in,"
a favourite mid-Victorian
pose used on postcards
and in advertising

75.
The "silver darlings"
off the East Neuk, 1910

76. Phoebe Holland, a well-known fishwife, Anstruther, 1900

77. North Fife Horticultural Society gathering, Luthrie, 1899

78. Haymaking on a Cupar farm, 1910

79. Mary Rollo, Cupar, making butter, 1898

80.
Sowing the old-
fashioned way at
Ceres, c. 1890

81.
Thomas Berwick in
the Botanic Gardens,
St Andrews, 1893

82.
Easter Forret, 1900.
William Rollo on
the binder.

83. The horse has always played a large part in Fife life and leisure.
Dappled-grey horses on a Falkland farm, 1902.

84. Three teams of work horses with leaders on a Cupar farm, 1905. Note the fashioned haystacks.

85. Harvesting in the shadow of Macduff's Castle, East Wemyss. Note the lady's distinctive sunhat, once a common sight among East Fife fieldworkers.

87.
A tinker encampment
at an East Wemyss
plantation, 1910

88.
Mending pans
and making metal
household goods,
East Wemyss, 1910

86. The knife grinder, outside Holy Trinity Church, St Andrews, c. 1890

89. Cardy net factory, Lower Largo, 1885. Note the ghostly dog! The factory was opened in 1868 and closed in 1886 after the collapse of the herring industry. The factory employed 60 girls, some of whom walked from Buckhaven (a round trip of some 14 miles) to begin work at seven o'clock. The factory is still intact and remains a fine example of Victorian Fife building and furbishing.

90. A village market, West Fife, c. 1900. Note the "carriage boat."

91. A horse fair at Ceres, c. 1905

92. William Mitchell of Cupar, thought to be the last clay pipe maker in Fife. The clay pipe industry was established in Cupar around the 1870s. The main site was at John Burton's premises at Back Lebanon, but the industry was started in Wedgin Close, Bonnygate. Mitchell worked for the Burton family and made pipes for over 65 years.

CHAPTER FOUR

SHIPS AND THE SEA

AN enduring eye-catching feature of the Fife ports in Victorian and Edwardian times was undoubtedly the sailing ship. Throughout the nineteenth century more and more efficient sailing ships were produced. Most of those calling at Fife ports were the wooden-hulled iron-framed clippers with half-iron masts. By 1838 Fife ports had been linked, by these vessels, with Orkney and Shetland, and by the 1850s sailing ships from Fife were running a mail service to Scandinavia. From 1867 to its heyday in 1877, East Neuk vessels were transporting coal to such places as Amsterdam.

The early nineteenth century in particular saw great developments in port facilities in Fife. The east coast linen industry naturally was to help develop the economic growth of Fife ports, as did the linoleum and coal industries which lay along the shores of Fife. As the railways became more expansive the ports declined, but exports of Fife coal kept shipping viable; so much so that there was a continued development of Fife docking piers from the 1870s up to the outbreak of World War I.

These were, of course, the days of the private mine owners who one way and another sank a great deal of money into Fife's seagoing life. Methil docks, for instance, was improved 1872-75. Prominent local families like that of Randolph Gordon Erskine Wemyss of Castle Wemyss did much to expand the dock facilities of West Wemyss, Methil and Leven.

Ships were built in Fife in mid-Victorian days. Two firms were active in Tayport by 1869. Newburgh had a yard and there were others at Dysart, Kinghorn, Limekilns and Inverkeithing. A prize was the 2645 ton steamer *Scotland* built by Keys of Kinghorn. The Scrimgeour yard at Newburgh built the famous brigantines *Leander* and *Racer* also at this time.

Pleasure steamers were all the rage along the Fife coast in high summer. There were ferries to and from the county at, for instance, Queensferry (for Edinburgh) and Ferryport-on-Craig (or Tayport—for Dundee).

By far the greatest number of boats to be seen in Fife waters were those associated with the herring trade. Most of the boats were the hazardous open vessels with no protective decking: the most famous were those of the larger type known as "Skaffies." By and large the Fife fishermen owned their own boats.

From the early years of Victoria's day seabathing became popular and the seaside holiday developed apace. Not everyone approved of what was called the "midsummer madness" of the Fife sands. There were angry letters in newspapers, and such august bodies as the Temperance League expressed concern about the indelicate way in which bathing was conducted on the West Sands, St Andrews, and the beaches of the East Neuk. Ladies frolicked about in the sea, and even danced polkas and posed for photographs in their bathing dresses. Nude bathing was not uncommon. Today we have come full circle as naturists petition to use the Fife beaches again!

93. Captain and first mate of the steamship *Carlyle*, in the Tay. Steamshipping between the Tay and London
began in 1826, with the activities of the Dundee Perth and London Shipping Co. The London run took six
days. Sometimes the competition for passengers was so keen that rival crews from Fife shore and Dundee shore
came to blows. Steamships around the Fife coast had a heyday c. 1870-80.

94. Paddle steamer on the Tay, c. 1890

95. Fishing-boat gala, East Wemyss, 1900

96. Anstruther fishing-boat, 1895

97. *HMS Mars* towed to berth near Newport

98. Kirkcaldy Harbour, c. 1890

99. Auld Bucket Pans, 1900. Originally they were pans where salt was gathered.

100. Foreshore of Redburn Wynd, Kirkcaldy, 1895

101. Dysart harbour and shipyard, with St Serf's tower. The village was once known as "Little Holland" in the days when coal, salt, beer and cured fish were exported. 1890.

102. West Sands, St Andrews, 1898

103. Beach Belles, St Andrews, 1909

104.   Passengers board a pleasure steamer, c. 1890. St Andrews Pier.

CHAPTER FIVE

SPECIAL OCCASIONS

SCOTLAND'S moments of glory and special occasions have often been tinged with tragedy; accidents robbing the country of its fame and social status alongside its Anglo-Saxon neighbour. Scotland, for instance, might have been the scene of the first Royal Command Variety Performance but for an accident. At the time, Edward VII and his entourage were at Balmoral, and the performance's organiser Sir Edward Moss was set to encourage the royals to attend the show en masse at Edinburgh. On May 9, 1911 Edward Moss's three-thousand seat Empire Palace burnt down. Moss never recovered from the shock and died five months later.

Many another Scottish accident was to make the headlines. In 1871 the foundation stone was laid for the railway bridge linking Fife and Angus. In 1877, the first train crossed from Wormit, on Fife shore, to Dundee. Alas, the bridge was to be doomed through poor workmanship. Unable to stand the wind pressure of a great gale, it collapsed (plate 115); on that night in December 1879 the eighty-eight feet high navigation span gave way taking with it a train (plate 105) and seventy-five lives. Yet, Scotland's Victorian society was vital to say the least and another new and more substantial bridge was erected over the Tay by 1887.

The heavy, romantic gloom of Victoriana in Scotland is splendidly epitomised by the vast city cemeteries. The Victorians produced more funeral paraphernalia—from mourning cards to crêpe hat bands—than any other generation. So no collection of photographs of the period would be complete without a funeral picture (plate 116). Indeed Scotland's cemeteries of Victorian vintage offer some of the era's finest works of art and some vital insights into the spirit of the age.

Victorian and Edwardian special occasions were not all gloomy. Amid the plethora of foundation stone layings, water works openings (plate 111) and processions were many excuses to be colourful. Flower shows were popular (plate 112) and gardening became a respectable and fashionable pursuit (even if the well-dressed middle class actually didn't turn a sod themselves!). It was the era of the public park, for the viewing of plant specimens and for the playing of "decorous games."

By the end of Victoria's reign it was popular to have works outings to public parks. Among the grandest were those sponsored by Sir Michael B. Nairn (1838-1915), the Kirkcaldy manufacturer. His public donations of a town school (1894) and a hospital (1890) were accompanied by suitable junketings.

Indeed Scotland's benefactors sponsored many a special occasion. Head and shoulders above them all, of course, was the Dunfermline-born industrialist Andrew Carnegie (1835-1919). His munificent gifts for Free Libraries, educational work, and charitable objects are well known (plate 113).

To the basically unsophisticated Fife society of 1837-1910 any relief from the toil of Victorian industrialisation was a special event. So the coming of a circus to town (plate 107) was a great occasion. Messrs Barnum and Bailey were to visit rural towns from 1871.

105.   The Wheatley bogie **224** at Cowlairs after recovery following the
Tay Bridge disaster. Refitted, 224 worked until 1924.

106. Moving the Roman Catholic church from the Scores, St Andrews, 1909. Some 55ft by 32ft, the shell of the building is buried at the corner of South Bridge Street and James Street.

107. The circus arrives at Cupar, 1899

108. Tramways were introduced to Kirkcaldy in 1903; the link
was extended to Leven in 1910.

109.
Proclamation of
Edward VII,
Kirkcaldy, 1901

110.
Kirkcaldy New Dock,
cutting the railway,
August 1, 1901

111. Ladybank Water Supply, Opening Ceremony

112. Flower Show, Dunfermline, 1899

113. Laying the foundation stone of the Carnegie Library, Dunfermline.
In 1880 Carnegie gave £8000 for the founding of a public library.

114.
Street procession
in Dunfermline, 1900.
Such outings were common
at the turn of the century,
both sacred and secular.

115. Tay Bridge from the Fife side, after the accident of 1879

117. "Tammy Polisher," 1888. He worked for many
years with Provost Macgregor, of John
Macgregor Ltd, St Andrews.

◄ 116. Funeral of Tom Morris, May 23, 1908

CHAPTER SIX

EDUCATION

WHEN Victoria's reign began, private schools grew apace in Fife to challenge the burgh schools. In Kirkcaldy alone, by 1845, there were 15 private schools in active competition with the Burgh School. Good subscription schools had also been established in Sinclairstown and Linktown. The same pattern was to be seen in Dunfermline which could also support the type of academic education for which Scotland had long been renowned.

In the Education (Scotland) Act of 1872, the state, for the first time, accepted the direct responsibility for educating children. Yet the admininstration of the schools still remained in the parishes or burghs in the form of ratepayer-elected school boards. Many church schools remained autonomous, but were self-funding. Teachers were appointed by these school boards which paid salaries levied from the local rates. Should parents be unable to pay the two or three pence a week school fees they could apply to the parochial board for poor relief. Before the Act the education of poor children in Fife was subject to private munificence, by such as Bailie Philp of Kirkcaldy. In country areas the lord of the manor often paid for communal school books.

The bright academic star in the Victorian and Edwardian night sky of education in Fife was St Andrews University. The great panjandrum of the academic scene at the beginning of Victoria's reign was scientist Sir David Brewster. He had addressed his famous *Letters on Natural Magic* to Sir Walter Scott, and encouraged early photography in Scotland. Brewster was to be remembered as the tactless, temperamental and dictatorial man, who yanked the university from its Georgian sleep into the Victorian noonday. The university was to have many financial problems during Victoria's day, but when her son's reign dawned the university had entered a new age of invigoration and redevelopment.

St Andrews was to benefit too, from the educational generosity of Dr Andrew Bell, man of letters and erstwhile tobacco trader. Bell devised the Madras, or monitorial system of education, and spent a large part of his considerable fortune in erecting Madras College, St Andrews, in 1832. The architect was William Burn of Edinburgh, who was to become one of the leading exponents of the Gothic Revival in Scotland. Madras College is of Jacobean style with Georgian inspiration (plate 121).

Wider powers were given to school boards by the Education (Scotland) Act of 1908. Now school boards could supervise medical care for children at school, and prosecute parents whose children were dirty or verminous, or were unable to attend for education because of lack of clothes or proper sustenance. Dunfermline was the first Scottish burgh to provide free medical treatment for school children, with the help of the College of Hygiene and Physical Education founded in Dunfermline in 1905 by the Carnegie Trust.

By and large, and in the context of its time, the education system in Edwardian Scotland was competent and progressive.

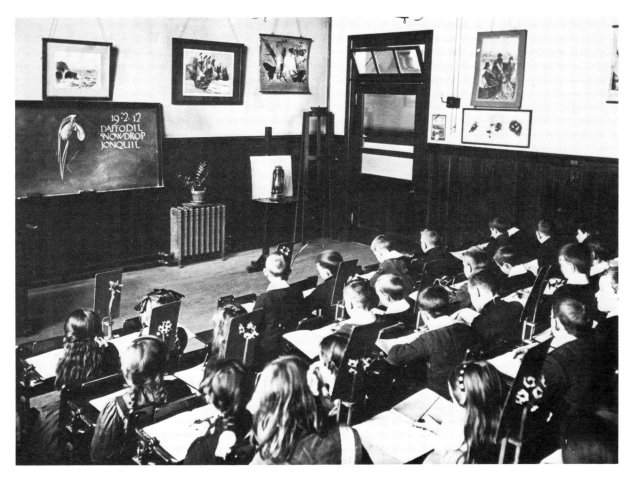

118. Children in an art class, Dunfermline

119.   A sewing class in a Dunfermline primary school, 1910

120. Pupils from Strathkiness School, c. 1900. Note the hobnailed boots—worn even by girls!—and the bare feet. This is perhaps the earliest rural school group photographed in Fife.

121. Madras school, St Andrews, in mid-Victorian times

122. Professor J.F. Ferrier's class in Moral Philosophy, 1862-3 with Andrew Lang (1844-1912) on the professor's right (in light trousers). Lang was the first Gifford Lecturer in Natural Theology in the university and author of a history of St Andrews town and gown. He wrote these lines on St Andrews:

St Andrews by the Northern Sea,
A haunted town it is to me!
A little city, worn and grey,
The grey North Ocean girds it round,
And o'er the rocks and up the bay,
The long sea-rollers surge and sound.

And still the thin and biting spray
Drives down the melancholy street,
And still endure, and still decay,
Towers that the salt winds vainly beat.
Ghost-like and shadowy they stand
Dim mirrored in the west sea-sand.

CHAPTER SEVEN

TRANSPORT

WHEN Victoria came to the throne in 1837 a goodly proportion of Fife working folk had never been further than the boundaries of their parishes in their lives. Great distances were walked. A six to eight mile round trip to school was not unusual and some workers walked up to fifteen miles a day to earn their living. The coming of the railways to Fife changed all this. These are the most important events in the history of railways in Fife during Victoria's day:

1843: The North British Railway Company was created. They were to be great rivals with the Caledonian Railway in Fife, mostly to secure freighting.

1845: The Edinburgh and Northern Railway established a line from Burntisland across the county, via Ladybank. Branches to Cupar and Lindores were opened in 1847. Branches to Perth and Dunfermline were established in 1848. This company was to become the Edinburgh, Perth and Dundee Railway in 1849 and was to dominate transport in Fife. The East Neuk Railway was to develop after 1859.

1846: The Caledonian Railway began to put pressure on the NBR for freight traffic. With the coming of the railway, Tayport became the southern terminus of the ferry service. The first railway in Kirkcaldy was formed in this year.

1877: The first train crossed from Fife to Angus.

1879: Tay Bridge disaster. (Bridge re-opened 1887).

1889: Randolph Wemyss sold his private railway at Methil to the NBR.

1890: Forth Rail Bridge opened.

The motor car industry dates from the perfection of the internal combustion engine by Nikolaus August Otto in 1876, and the patenting in 1885 by Gottlieb Daimler of a single-cylinder high-speed engine.

In 1896 the notorious "Red Flag Act" (which imposed a strict speed limit for cars, each having to have a man preceding it on foot holding a red warning flag) was replaced by the Locomotives and Highways Act, and the maximum speed limit on Fife roads was now fixed at 14 mph. The speed was raised to 20 mph in 1904 when it became compulsory for cars to have number plates.

Doctors were among the first professional men in Fife to use motor cars, as were prosperous traders and industrialists. A new job was now open to the adventurous Fifer, that of chauffeur. Every wealthy man had his own car, following the lead of the King himself; most people tried to buy a Daimler, a Renault or a Mercedes to be like the King. Up to 1906 petrol was only available in Kirkcaldy.

For the ordinary folk in Fife the most popular means of road transport was the bicycle. The pneumatic tyre was "re-invented" (it had first appeared in 1846) by J. B. Dunlop, giving the bicycle a great step forward. 1896-97 were boom years for the bicycle in Fife. Thanks to the bicycle the female ankle made its appearance in public, for women's fashions rapidly took in the needs of the cyclist. The machines also brought a greater freedom in courtship for cycle clubs gave men and women "respectable" reasons for cycling together.

123. The travelling menagerie arrives at Kirkcaldy, 1890

124. A tramway was formed from Kirkcaldy to Leven in 1910. It was subsidised
by the Wemyss family and was called the Wemyss & District Tramway Co.

125. Trams competed with horse vehicles up to World War I. Trams were introduced to
Kirkcaldy in 1903 and were run by Kirkcaldy Corporation.

126. Horse-drawn bus at Falkland, c. 1905. Several Fife hoteliers, shaking their heads at the foolhardiness of using the motor car, retained carriages for their guests up to the beginning of World War I.

127. Three-wheeled traffic at the railway bridge, St Andrews, c. 1890. By the 1890s the pneumatic tyre, free-wheeling bicycle has superseded the penny farthing. Tricycles were suitable for ladies with long skirts.

128. Char-à-banc at Kirkcaldy, c. 1905. Kirkcaldy was one of the first centres used by visitors for the exploration of Fife.

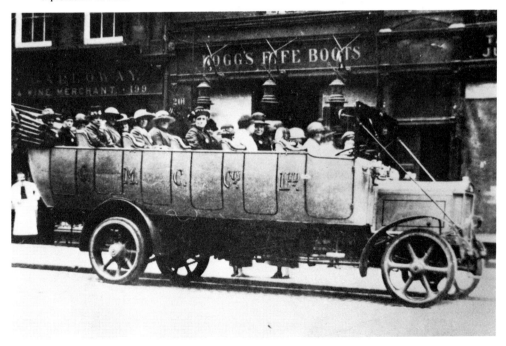

129.
An early Morris
car at Letham Post
Office, c. 1907

130.
Chauffeur with
estate car,
Mount Melville,
St Andrews, c. 1907

131. Two-way motorcycle, Freuchie, c. 1903

132. Largo's first car, c. 1906. Compulsory licence plates appeared in 1904.

133. James and John Christie outside their workshop at 55 South Street, St Andrews, 1909

134. Kirkcaldy Naturalist Society take a train trip on the Auchtertool line, 1880s

CHAPTER EIGHT

PASTIMES AND SPORTS

SPORTS tend to breed larger than life characters and heroes, and amongst the sporting paragons of Fife the "golfing greats" stand head and shoulders above the others. When on May 14, 1754 the twenty-two Fife noblemen and gentlemen formed themselves into "The Society of St Andrews Golfers," they were unleashing a sports enthusiasm which was to develop into a religion.

The famous Royal and Ancient Golf Club of St Andrews, so styled after King William IV's patronage of 1834, opened its clubhouse in 1854 and focussed attention on a golf course which has now become hallowed turf. King and commoner have posed and strutted here. Up to 1912 golf on St Andrews links was free of charge to all players: none more legendary than three golfers whose photographs appear here—Tom Morris (plate 145), Allan Robertson (plate 142) and Donald Blue (plate 144).

Tom Morris, "Old Tom," (1821-1908) supervised the Old Course green staff of two men, a barrow, a spade and a shovel from 1846. Allan Robertson (1815-59) was reputed to have been only twice beaten in singles, and then by "Old Tom." Playing together the duo were never beaten. In 1858 Robertson created a record for the Old Course of 79.

While the earliest illustration of curling is to be found in the Flemish painter Pieter Bruegel's winter scenes c. 1560, the club with the earliest records (c. 1716) is Kilsyth, Stirlingshire. It is likely that the sport was flourishing in Fife by the eighteenth century and was a popular county pastime in Victoria and Edward's days (plate 136). Football too was acceptable, but mostly at an amateur level (plate 141), as the professional teams did not really develop until after 1910. East Fife Football Club, for instance, though formed in 1903, was not made into a limited liability company until 1911.

The Fifer of Victoria's early days did not relish his pleasures, whether they were "booze and fun" at one end of the social scale, or horse-riding and grouse-shooting at the other. Travellers from the continent, like Heinrich Heine, saw drab monotony in the pastimes of middle-class Victorian Fife, and it seemed that the people had "troubled spirits even in pleasure itself." Calvinist conscience could just about allow nature rambles and walks in parks as worthy pastimes with the odd picnic basket thrown in—if not too ostentatious! As the era developed, however, the picnic became a mass pastime.

The picnics which seemed to have caused most joy were those from around 1840. The Sunday school was maintained zealously by the different Fife churches. Here for a few hours each week children, mostly from poverty-stricken homes, were taught in religious principles and reading. At certain times of the year, hoards of these children were hauled, in gaily decorated horse carts, to picnic sites on land and by sea. Each child was fed and watered and amused—a highlight being the adults' races where Sunday school teachers would compete.

135.   Guardbridge Papermill Rifle Team, 1905

137.
Decorating a horse
and waggon for
a Sunday School
picnic, c. 1903

138.
The Ladies' Race,
c. 1900

◄ 136. Curling, Kirkcaldy 1860

139. "Ye'll be needin' this if ye want a gemme!" c. 1900.

140. Feeding the ducks, Lower Largo, 1890s

141. St Andrews City Football Team, 1905

142. Allan Robertson, Golf Champion

143. Scotland's Ladies Golf Final, R & A Clubhouse, St Andrews.
Miss E. Grace Sutter (putting), I. L. Kyle (runner up).

144. Donald Blue, the most famous St Andrews caddie of his day

143. Scotland's Ladies Golf Final, R & A Clubhouse, St Andrews.
Miss E. Grace Sutter (putting), I. L. Kyle (runner up).

144.   Donald Blue, the most famous St Andrews caddie of his day

145.
Tom Morris,
golfer extraordinary,
c. 1900